W9-BFD-031

Nature
CLOSE-UPS
Nature

Spotlight on Spiders

-Text and photographs by Densey Clyne-

Gareth Stevens Publishing
MILWAUKEE

Tropical spiny spider

Words that appear in the glossary are printed in **boldface** type the first time they occur in the text.

Frightening or fascinating?

Huntsman spider

A monster from a horror movie . . . a killer creeping from a crevice with fangs poised to strike . . . death on eight hairy legs! That's what many people imagine when they think of spiders.

But spiders are often unjustly accused. For the most part, spiders do not deserve their negative reputation!

The colorful little spider *(below)* is not at all scary. Colorful spiders are usually small, making it easy for them to hide. Larger spiders tend to have dark or neutral coloring, which becomes natural **camouflage**.

Triangular spider

Hunters and fishers

Huntsman spider with its prey

The huntsman spider (*above*) has killed a large tree cricket. A spider must kill any large-sized **prey** quickly or the spider could be injured.

Nearly all spiders kill their victims by injecting poison through the tips of their **fangs**. The poison is stored in **glands** in the spider's head.

Spiders have silk glands at the back end of their body. Spinning and using silk sets spiders and some insects apart from all other animals.

An orb-weaving spider
at the center of its web

Spiders produce silk mainly for webs, of which
there are many kinds. The one (above) is an **orb**
web. The spider sits at the center of the web.
It lays a sticky spiral over the "spokes" in the
web to catch its prey.

A spider wraps its prey in silk.

The spider (*above*) has captured a cockroach in its web. The spider binds the insect with silk threads, then carries it back to the center of the web.

Spiders cannot eat solid food. All of their meals must be digested first. The spider fills the insect with digestive fluid from its mouth to dissolve the insect's internal parts.

The spider then sucks in the liquid meal. The insect's hard outer covering is too tough to dissolve and is discarded.

A Ulysses butterfly trapped in a golden orb-weaver's web

In Australia, the web of a spider called the golden orb-weaver is so strong it can trap tiny birds. These big spiders are sometimes called bird-eating spiders, although they do not try to catch the birds. The Ulysses butterfly (*above*) cannot escape and is a golden orb-weaver's next meal.

These spiders strengthen their huge, golden webs with a system of silk strands at the back.

This spider and honeybee are victims of one another.

Spiders have no control over what lands in their webs. Insects that are a danger to spiders, such as wasps and bees, must quickly be cut out of the sticky silk by the spider.

Caught in a web, a honeybee will fight to use its stinger to kill the spider. But when a honeybee stings, it dies as the stinger is pulled from its body. In this case, both **predator** and prey die (above).

Not all spiders use silk traps. Wolf spiders that live in Australia leave their **burrows** at night to hunt on the ground for insects.

Wolf spiders vary in size. They can often be seen searching for food on a summer's night.

Two of the wolf spider's eyes are much bigger than its other six eyes. This makes this spider easy to identify.

Wolf spider

Jumping spiders are found throughout the world, with the most colorful species living in the tropics. Like wolf spiders, two of their eight eyes are much larger than the rest.

Jumping spiders leap among leaves and branches, pouncing on small insects. If they miss their footing, they dangle safely on the silk thread trailing behind them.

Jumping spiders

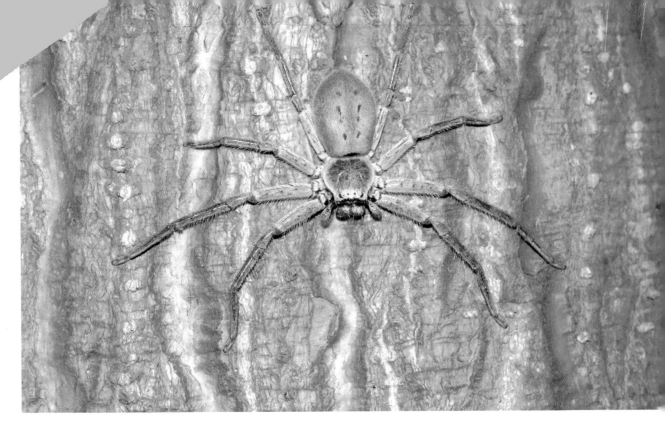

Huntsman spider on a tree trunk

Some spiders, such as the huntsman, are **ambushers**. Although they sometimes come indoors, their usual home is on a tree trunk. They hide under the bark by day and hunt for food at night.

Tree trunks are highways for insects that travel upward at night to feed among the leaves. They leave scent trails the spider can detect. After dark, the spider settles down near a trail and waits. When an insect comes by, the spider ambushes it for a meal.

A flower spider with its prey

Flower spiders eat butterflies and other **nectar**-feeding insects. They wait at the edge of a flower, well camouflaged and very, very still. When an insect settles to feed, the spider moves forward, stretches out its long front legs, and grabs.

Even tiny flowers can have a spider waiting inside.

A flower spider waits for a nectar-feeding insect.

Fishing spider

The fishing spider (*above*) lives around fresh-water ponds and creeks, preying on **aquatic** insects. It dives into the water after the insects. Fishing spiders even catch and eat small fish.

The hairs on the legs of these spiders act as life jackets. Air trapped in the hairs provides enough **buoyancy** to bring the spiders and their victims to the surface of the water.

14

A net-casting spider with its woolly net

The net-casting spider has keen vision.

The net-casting spider is also an ambusher, but it prepares a net of springy silk. This silk is unusual. Instead of being sticky, it is dense and woolly.

At night, the spider locates an insect trail. It hangs head-down with the net folded between its legs. When an insect comes near, the spider drops down on its safety line, expands the net to a much larger size, and wraps the victim in its folds.

This spider will have a tasty meal of a fly.

The spider (*above*) has caught a fly. It holds the fly by its head. To capture food, the spider sits on a leaf and waits for flies to approach.

The flies do not arrive just by chance, but scientists do not know for certain what attracts them.

Many flies are attracted to animal droppings and debris, and the spider could be mistaken for a substance of this sort.

The magnificent, or Bolas, spider spins a thread of sticky silk and dangles it like a fishing line. It eats only male moths of a certain kind. Moths find mates by scent, so the spider produces a scent that imitates a female moth's. When prey is near, the spider swings the silky thread in circles to trap the victim.

Inset: *A magnificent spider wraps its prey in silk.*

Above: *This magnificent spider dangles a "fishing line" to catch a moth.*

A funnelweb spider in its striking position

Ground-dwelling spiders, such as trapdoors and funnelwebs, have less complicated ways of catching their prey. These big, burrowing spiders form a special group of their own, and some of them are very poisonous.

Funnelweb and trapdoor spiders and their relatives have fangs that strike downward with great force. They carry a very potent poison. They are dangerous to humans because they can pierce human skin. Male funnelweb spiders have the most powerful poisons of the group.

Leaves and sticks disguise the entrance to a trapdoor spider's burrow.

Trapdoor spiders are stay-at-home ambushers. They wait at their burrow entrance for an insect to pass by, sensing the vibrations through their feet. Then they move as quickly as lightning to strike and secure their prey.

Most kinds of trapdoor spiders make silk-and-soil lids to disguise their burrows, but the one pictured does not. It binds leaves and sticks together with silk. The material is then placed around the burrow entrance.

Staying alive

Now you see it, now you don't!

Many spiders do disappearing acts to escape their enemies. Some vanish against a tree trunk. For example, the lichen spider in the picture (*above*) faces head down, making it difficult to see. Spiders at rest can look like a scrap of debris, a broken stem, even bird droppings — anything but a spider.

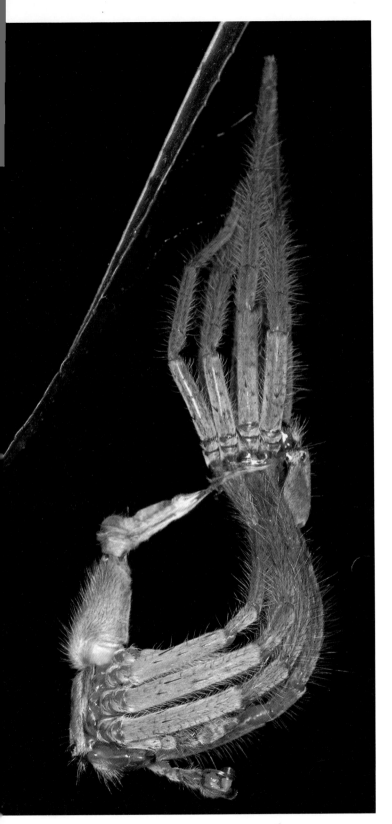

A huntsman spider casts off its old skin.

While a spider feeds and grows, its tough outer covering does not grow with it.

So every now and then before it is fully grown, it has to **molt**. With each molting, it casts off its entire skin.

This huntsman spider has nearly finished molting. Its body is free, but now it must carefully pull the "new" legs out of the "old" legs.

The spider will need to hide from danger while the new skin dries and becomes firm.

Mating — a dangerous game

A male orb-weaving spider courts a female.

A male orb-weaving spider approaches a female at the edge of her web. By twanging on her web, he persuades her to join him. He must show her through his **courtship behavior** that he is the right **mate** for her. Otherwise, she might mistake him for a meal!

Courtship is unique to each kind of spider, and females respond only to males of their own kind. Spider courtship takes time and patience.

22

A tiny male St. Andrew's cross spider with his giant mate

A male St. Andrew's cross spider must be careful during mating because he is much smaller than his mate. In fact, mating is often the last thing he does before he dies. Most male St. Andrew's cross spiders die soon after.

A new generation

A net-casting spider makes an egg sac.

For female spiders, mating begins the long and complex job of egg-laying. Once the female has laid her eggs, she encloses them in an egg sac, a protective covering of many layers of silk. This net-casting spider (*above*) has built up many layers of silk around her mass of eggs.

Egg sacs are made in different shapes by different spiders. For safety, spiders disguise their sacs with leaves.

Above: *A magnificent spider makes an egg sac.*

Right: *The completed egg sacs*

Glands in the female spiders' bodies produce silk for the sac. The silk inside it is loosely woven for **insulation**. The silk outside is closely woven for protection.

A female wolf spider drags her egg sac.

Wolf spiders live in burrows and hunt at night. Instead of leaving the egg sac behind when she goes hunting, the female wolf spider takes it with her. She drags the large egg sac along, attached to her **spinnerets**.

When wolf spider eggs hatch, the babies ride piggyback on their mother. As she chases after prey, they cling tightly to the hairs on her back.

Huntsman spider with spiderlings

Many other spider mothers practice tender loving care with their **offspring**.

The female huntsman's spider makes her egg sac beneath the tree bark where she lives. While the eggs are developing inside, the mother wraps her legs around the egg sac and will not leave it.

In the picture (*above*), the spiderlings clustered around their mother are not there just for safety. The huntsman mother shares her meals with the offspring. They crowd around and eat with her.

Silk supports these spiderlings after they hatch.

Fresh out of the protective egg sac, spiderlings already know how to produce silk and what to do with it. For starters, they use it for support and safety as they cluster together.

Next, they must cast off the skins they were hatched in. They already had their first molt inside the egg sac.

Then it's out into the big world. They will scatter far and wide to live in the way they are meant to, whether by web-making, ambushing, hunting, fishing, or playing tricks on insects.

Friend or foe?

Spiders live all around us in great numbers. Where insects exist, there are also spiders to keep their numbers limited. And think of this — spiders have been around for more than 400 million years!

How should we think of the spiders that share our world? Are they evil monsters and creepy killers? They are more likely diverse and fascinating animals worthy of respect.

Glossary

ambusher: one who attacks by surprise from a hiding place.

aquatic: living in or growing in the water.

buoyancy: the ability to float.

burrow: a hole dug in the ground by a small animal for its home.

camouflage: a way of disguising something or someone to make it look like its surroundings. An animal's camouflage helps it blend in with its habitat.

courtship behavior: actions undertaken for the purpose of gaining a mate.

fang: a poison-containing part of a spider's body.

gland: an organ in the body that manufactures certain substances for accomplishing tasks.

insulation: a material that slows or prevents heat or cold from passing through.

mate (v): to join together to produce young.

molt: to shed an outer covering, such as feathers, hair, or skin.

nectar: the sweet liquid produced by flowers that attracts bees, birds, and other animals.

offspring: the young of an animal.

orb: a circular object.

predator: an animal that hunts other animals for food.

prey: an animal that is hunted for food by other animals.

spinneret: an organ in a spider's body that produces threads of silk.

Books to Read

Amazing Spiders. Claudia Schneiper (Carolrhoda)

Animal Survival (series). Michel Barré (Gareth Stevens)

Discovering Spiders. Malcolm Perry (Watts)

Eight Legs. D.M. Souza (Carolrhoda)

Insects and Spiders. Lorus J. Milne and Margery Milne (Doubleday)

The New Creepy Crawly Collection (series). (Gareth Stevens)

Spiders: The Great Spinners. Secrets of the Animal World (series). Andreu Llamas (Gareth Stevens)

Young Naturalist Field Guides (series). (Gareth Stevens)

Videos

Animals and Arachnids. (Moonbeam)

Insects and Spiders. (Kimbo)

Meet Your Animal Friends. (Library Video)

Protective Coloration. (Coronet/Multimedia)

See How They Grow: Insects and Spiders. (Sony)

Tell Me Why: Animals and Arachnids. (Prism)

Web Sites

www.mtco.com/~brent/spider.htm

dns.ufsia.ac.be/Arachnology/Arachnology.html

www.xs4all.nl/~ednieuw/Spiders/spidhome.htm

spiders.arizona.edu/

Index

burrows 10, 18, 19, 26

camouflage 4, 13

digestion 7

eggs/egg sacs 24, 25, 26, 27, 28
eyes 10, 11

fangs 5, 18
fishing spiders 14
funnelweb spiders 18

glands, silk 5, 25
golden orb-weavers 8, 22

huntsman spiders 3, 5, 12, 21, 27

magnificent (Bolas) spiders 17, 25
mating 22, 23, 24
molting 21, 28

net-casting spiders 15, 24

orb web 6

poison 5, 18

silk 5, 6, 7, 8, 9, 10, 11, 15, 17, 19, 24, 25, 28
skin 18, 21, 28

spiderlings 27, 28
spinnerets 26
St. Andrew's cross spiders 23

trapdoor spiders 18, 19
triangular spiders 4
tropical spiny spiders 2

webs 6, 7, 8, 9, 22, 28
wolf spiders 10, 11, 26

For a free color catalog describing Gareth Stevens Publishing's list of high-quality books and multimedia programs, call 1-800-542-2595 (USA) or 1-800-461-9120 (Canada). Gareth Stevens Publishing's Fax: (414) 225-0377. See our catalog, too, on the World Wide Web: http://gsinc.com

The publisher would like to extend special thanks to Jan W. Rafert, Curator of Primates and Small Mammals, Milwaukee County Zoo, Milwaukee, Wisconsin, for his kind and professional help with the information in this book.

Library of Congress Cataloging-in-Publication Data

Clyne, Densey.
    Spotlight on spiders / by Densey Clyne.
        p. cm. — (Nature close-ups)
    "First published in 1995 by Allen & Unwin Pty Ltd . . . Australia" — T.p. verso.
    Includes bibliographical references and index.
    Summary: Examines how spiders find their food, defend themselves against danger, and protect their eggs.
    ISBN 0-8368-2061-4 (lib. bdg.)
    1. Spiders—Juvenile literature.
[1. Spiders.] I. Title. II. Series: Clyne, Densey. Nature close-ups.
QL458.4.C59   1998
595.4'4—dc21   97-31733

First published in North America in 1998 by
Gareth Stevens Publishing
1555 North RiverCenter Drive
Suite 201
Milwaukee, WI 53212 USA

First published in 1995 by Allen & Unwin Pty Ltd, 9 Atchison Street, St. Leonards, NSW 2065, Australia.

Text and photographs © 1995 by Densey Clyne. Additional end matter © 1998 by Gareth Stevens, Inc.

Printed in the United States of America

1 2 3 4 5 6 7 8 9 02 01 00 99 98